Commercial Voice Over Strategies

VOICE OVER AND VOICE ACTING

Commercial Voice Over Strategies

TELL A STORY, LAND THE JOB

CHRIS AGOS

Published by www.complete-voiceover.com

© 2020 Chris Agos All rights reserved.

No part of this publication may be reproduced, stored in a retrieval system, or transmitted in any form or by any means, electronic, mechanical, photocopying, recording or otherwise, without the prior written permission of the publisher. For permission, contact the publisher at publisher at info@complete-voiceover.com.

Disclaimer of Warranty, Limitation of Liability. Neither the publisher nor the author make any representations or warranties with respect to the accuracy or completeness of the contents of this work; and they specifically disclaim all warranties, whether express or implied, including without limitation fitness for a particular purpose. No warranty may be created or extended by sales or promotional materials. Nothing contained in this work is to be considered as the rendering of legal, accounting or other professional advice for specific cases, and readers are responsible for obtaining such advice from their own professional counsel. Neither the publisher nor the author will be liable for any loss, damage or injury arising from or related to this work. The fact that an organization or website may be referenced in this work does not mean that the author or the publisher endorses the information that such organization or website may provide or any recommendations it may make. Further, readers should be aware that Internet websites listed in this work may have changed or vanished between this work's creation and when it is read; and neither the author nor the publisher are responsible for any such websites (or their content). Unless expressly stated, the author has received no compensation for any products and services mentioned herein. All product and company names are trademarks™ or registered® trademarks of their respective holders. Use of them does not imply any affiliation with or endorsement by them.

ISBN: 978-0-9828863-8-0

For free voice acting lessons, visit

www.Complete-Voiceover.com

About Chris Agos

Chris Agos launched his acting and voice over career in 1995. As a voice talent, Chris quickly developed a reputation for efficiency and professionalism, resulting in a career spanning thousands of projects from commercials to corporate to narration and beyond.

As an on-camera actor, he appears in TV shows across various networks and streaming services. Chris has taught voice acting since 2007 and has authored a number of books on the subject, helping talent aim for the highest levels of the industry by taking a big-picture view of each project and magnifying it with storytelling.

He continues to audition, work, and help others get what they want from their voice over and acting careers. A Chicago native, he lives in Los Angeles with his wife and twin sons.

Twitter: @ChrisAgos
Instagram: @ChrisAgos
YouTube: https://www.youtube.com/ChrisAgosActor
IMDb: https://imdb.me/ChrisAgos

Visit **Complete-Voiceover.com** for videos and books on voice over and voice acting.

Visit **ChrisAgos.com** for reels and demos.

Visit **ActingInChicago.com** for info on acting in the Midwest, USA.

Other books from complete-voiceover.com

The Voice Over Startup Guide: How to Land Your First VO Job

Voice Over and Voice Acting: Movie Trailer Mastery

Acting In Chicago: Making a Living in Commercials, Voice Over, TV/Film and More

Get The Audio

We've put together a collection of audio files to go along with examples in this book. They're available to download for free at Complete-Voiceover.com. The link is at the top of the home page.

Reading about voice over is great, but your learning will be much more complete if you also hear examples of voice over work.

We recommend first saving the files to your computer. From there you can transfer them to your tablet, phone, or any other device. They are .mp3 files, so you can import them into a sound editor or even burn them to a CD. If you need technical support, please email us via the site's contact form.

Kindle/eReaders

To get the most out of this book, turn off column viewing and hold your Kindle in landscape mode.

Get your audio now for free. You'll learn so much more if you do!

www.Complete-Voiceover.com

Introduction

You may have heard that the TV commercial is dying. You have heard wrong.

It's true that streaming networks have changed the way we watch TV, but the broadcast and cable networks still need advertising to fund their programming, and they're not going anywhere. Add in the explosion in short-form online commercials seen on every major platform, and it's obvious commercials are not dead by a long shot.

This is great news because commercials just might be the voice actor's perfect job. Commercials, or spots as they're called in ad industry jargon, provide two things that are critical to having a voice over (VO) career: visibility and cash flow.

Booking a commercial literally broadcasts your brand (your voice) to thousands of potential employers. Any voice actor who has done them will say that commercials can be far more lucrative than just about any other VO genre. You might love voice over enough to do it for free, but even the most excited among us eventually has to earn a living.

Given the benefits, how can we do more commercials? We can have amazing recording gear, fantastic agents, and mind-blowing voice demos, but those things don't matter nearly as much as your ability to interpret and deliver commercial scripts.

It all begins and ends with you. By reading this book, you've made a great decision. You've chosen to aim for the high end of today's competitive

Introduction

commercial marketplace. My goal is to give you tools to deliver insightful, captivatingly original reads that make decision makers stop and think when they hear them.

You'll learn how to take a big-picture view of the spot before you even speak a word of it. We'll talk about the importance of identifying what commercials are actually selling. Then we'll dive into specific examples and break down high-quality scripts into their respective parts. Those sample scripts (the ad world calls these "copy") are based on actual spots that made it to air.

When you speak for a brand, no matter how large or small, creatives will listen.

Why the emphasis on copy interpretation and delivery? There are a lot of moving parts to voice over, and we sometimes feel like something's missing. We think we would work more if we only had better tools or industry relationships. Those are part of the equation, but they can certainly let you down. Your mic may not be the best choice for your voice. Your agent may lose interest in you. But your ability will never let you down. If you put up a great read, you cannot be ignored.

Today's ad agency creatives (the people who came up with the spot's concept) have lofty expectations for "realness." They want you to sound like you've never done voice over before, yet they also want you to take direction in the session, something that's nearly impossible unless–you guessed it–you've done voice over before. To pull this off, you have to be great with copy. This is true at all levels of commercial work, from the local furniture store's thirty-second spot to the six-second YouTube preroll for a consumer brand to the two-minute pharmaceutical commercial. It's true whether you're union (SAG-AFTRA) or not, new to the business or a seasoned pro, signed with an agent or working solo.

What you're about to read is based on my years of observing, listening to, and performing

Introduction

in commercials. To date, I've done about fifteen hundred of them in every tier of the business. I've lent my voice to everything from mom-and-pop stores to global brands occupying a spot in the top ten advertisers by spend. I've been around. But my way of doing things is just one path to a great commercial read. I don't have all the answers, and I'm still learning every day. I'm just happy to share what I've learned thus far.

A lot of my friends and former students also apply this kind of thinking to their commercial work. Why? Because it works. I encourage you to keep an open mind if our suggestions differ from what you've been taught before.

There are a lot of variables in the world of VO. No one should promise you'll make a certain amount of money if you do things their way. I certainly won't. But I will promise this: all my years of listening, questioning, learning, writing, teaching, directing, and taking direction are here, ready for you to absorb. I left nothing out.

When you finish reading, I think you'll decide it was a great investment. Let's get busy.

CHAPTER ONE

Landing the Job

Who's booking commercials these days? The short answer is this: the VO talent who makes decision makers feel what they expect to feel when they hear the read.

I think it's worth hearing the long answer. A lot goes into a casting decision, and no two jobs are cast in the same way because no two creative teams (the writers and creative directors in charge of producing the spot) are the same. One team might have more of an idea of what they want than another. Some teams might be united in their vision for the VO, while others could be divided.

One thing is certain: by the time the script is sent out for an audition, they've lived with that spot for a long time. They know what they want when they hear it. Understanding this dynamic starts with knowing how a spot gets made and where the voice talent fits in.

Here's a simplified description of the process: a commercial starts with a product or service that needs some publicity. Let's say it's a new car. The car manufacturer hires an advertising agency to market the car. The ad agency people talk with the car company people about what kind of image the car should have, who might be the target buyer, and other things that will shape the look and feel of the advertising. Then the ad agency people go back to their office and come up with a few ideas for the car company to look at. When the client hears a concept they like, commercial scripts are written and submitted for approval.

Let's say a commercial gets greenlit for production. The ad agency then hires a firm that specializes in the production of commercials, called a production company. Those folks work with the ad agency to make sure the spot comes out exactly as it was pitched to and approved by the car company.

The spot is shot, edited together, color treated, and enhanced with visual effects and/or graphics. Music is written or licensed, and finally, someone will think about the voice over. The creative team talks with the client about the kind of voice they think the spot requires. They might know exactly what they want, or they might be open to a range of genders, ages, and ethnicities. Depending on the spot's budget, a casting director might be hired to find the voice talent, or the ad agency might go directly to talent agents and ask them to have people on their roster audition for the job. Once the creative team hears a couple voices they like, they'll probably run their top choice past the client, who will likely have the final say on who ultimately lands the booking.

That describes a high-budget production undertaken by a large national brand. What about clients with smaller budgets? The process will be the same, albeit with fewer steps, and when it comes to casting, they might be willing to take more risks. Instead of putting out an audition, the ad agency might ask a few talent who have done other work for the agency to read for the job. Or they might post the audition on a VO membership site. In any case, the list of potential voices could be in the hundreds. The voice is usually the last thing added to the edit, and the casting decisions are almost always made by committee. Once the spot is approved, it'll be aired and retired when it's no longer needed.

Complementing the Story

In the end, the whole of the spot will add up to more than the sum of its parts. Here's an analogy. My wife puts way more thought into how she looks than I do. If we're going to a party, before she thinks about what she's going to wear, she considers what kind of party it is, what time of day it's being held, the party's location, and who's going to be there.

Then she thinks about what kind of statement she wants to make. Does she want to stand out or blend in? Is there some etiquette involved, like not wearing white to a wedding? What's the weather going to be like? Only after she has all of those answers will she look through her closet and put together a look. She picks clothes, then shoes, then jewelry and accessories, and does her hair and makeup. Then when we're late, she'll be ready to leave (sorry, honey, I had to).

This is a lot like how talent buyers choose their VO talent. The choice that's made has to fit into the bigger picture. The wrong choice can ruin the whole thing.

Copywriters, creative directors, and clients all consider the world of the spot and pick a voice that would live in it. Certain things, like the amount of texture in the voice, are like a pair of boots in my wife's closet. While she might wonder if they go with the rest of her look, creatives will wonder, "Does that voice have too much texture, or should we go with one that's more polished?"

Since the voice over is part of the larger story, it must serve that story, and in the end the talent that serves it best gets the booking. The voice has to be the right gender and age and have the right blend of vocal quality and copy interpretation to fit with the ad's concept.

This is good to keep in mind. It means there's no one thing that will get you any particular job. If you're used to focusing on one aspect of your reads, you now know it's a combination of factors that gets you work. While you do have to nail some things, there are many, many factors that are out of your control.

And that leads us to the point of all this: your main concern should be to work on your reads. Control what you can control. You can vocally match up with what the agency is looking for, but if you can't come as close as possible to the read the creatives imagine in their heads, you're not booking the job.

Feelings, Nothing More Than Feelings

I want to go back to this idea that the decision makers need to feel something in order to book a voice actor. This is evidenced by the language creatives use. They won't say, "The voice is going too fast on this line." Instead, they'll say, "It feels like the voice is rushing." They're not going to say, "The talent's talking too loudly." Instead, they'll be like, "I feel like he's not connecting. He's too announcery." There's an emotional component to their comments because they're hoping to respond to the read on that level.

As voice talent auditioning for a job, we need to make decision makers feel two things. First, that we understand what they're trying to do with the spot. This is universally true no matter the job. If you can't convince them that you get what they're going for, you're out.

Secondly, we need to make talent buyers feel how they want their intended audience to feel. Uplifted? Inspired? Do they want to laugh? Whatever the spot calls for. This is hard, but we've got one important thing going for us: they *want* you to make them feel something. Believe me, every creative listening to your audition is rooting for you. Why? Because they need you.

Everyone who works on a spot is auditioning for someone else. You're reading for the job, but the person listening to your read wants to recommend the right voice talent. Professionally, their taste and understanding of the spot is on trial. Choosing the wrong voice makes them look bad. They need to do a good job for their team, and the team needs to do their best work for the client. The only way that happens is if all the elements of the spot line up exactly as intended, voice included.

How do we make them feel these things? Helping them see that we understand the spot is easy. Writers leave us clues that add up to something we've probably seen before. There are no new ideas; you've seen every type of commercial a thousand times. We'll go over this in a bit, but once you've been doing this awhile, you'll be able to quickly understand what kind of spot you're dealing with.

Making them feel what they hope to make viewers feel is a little trickier. But if you take a big-picture view of the script, then dive into the different parts of it, you're well on your way. Some scripts make this easy, others not so much, but in the coming pages, you'll see and hear what I mean.

Chapter Two

We Don't Sell Stuff

There's something about commercials that's counterintuitive, but critical for voice talent to understand. Commercials don't sell stuff. Truck commercials don't sell trucks, insurance commercials don't sell insurance, and so on.

Commercials sell ways of being and states of mind. Security, happiness, confidence, fun, awareness, togetherness, family, pride, urgency, gratitude, sometimes fear. What marketers really want you to do isn't necessarily go out and buy a truck, although if you did, they'd be fine with that. But they're smart enough to know most people aren't going to make a purchase just because they saw a commercial, so they hope for the next best thing. They want to connect their brand to the way you feel. And they never, ever want you to be sad. They want you to be happy.

Let's take a look at some examples. Head to www.**complete-voiceover.com**, and click on the audio downloads link at the top of the page. Find the book you're reading and download the zip file. When you open it, you'll find a bunch of mp3s that match the examples in the book. There's also a clickable list of the following examples if you need it. Some of the example don't have a voice over, but they're all great for illustrating what I mean when I say that commercials sell ways of being and states of mind.

Keep in mind that at the time of writing, the example links were current and available, yet by the time you read this, they may not be. If you encounter dead links, just search for the brand and description of the spot, and you should be able to find it. Other than having a channel, I'm not affiliated with YouTube, and I have no connection with iSpot.tv, a data analytics company for the ad industry. But I do like to use them for research.

Safety and Security

Marketers would love it if you associated their brand with your safety and security. In an uncertain world, it feels good to know that if we make the right choice, we're going to be taken care of. This strategy personalizes a brand, so when it's time to make a choice about a product, we're more likely to consider theirs.

Example 2a

>Apple – "Get A Mac – Viruses"
>
>This classic campaign from Apple aimed to settle a debate that was raging at the time:

Which is better, Mac or PC? The audience is going to laugh because this spot is hilarious, but it also makes you feel like when you choose a Mac, you're going to be just fine.

https://youtu.be/n8aXFqL3RIQ

Example 2b

P&G – "Thank You Mom"

The consumer products giant has been sponsoring the Olympic Games for years, and their "Proud Sponsor of Moms" campaign tells lovely stories of mothers supporting their kids. They tug our heartstrings using emotion and nostalgia, and we come away thinking about times in our own lives when we were nurtured by someone. That's a much bigger idea than any one consumer product. The VO at the end supports the story with a very warm read.

https://www.youtube.com/watch?v=bQoJqDi8490

Example 2c

OHSU – "Make Cancer the Victim"

This spot for a university uses VO to tell the story of their successful treatment of a type of cancer. Sure, they wouldn't mind if patients thought of them first if they need treatment, but what this spot is really trying to help you understand is that if you ever need them, they'll be there for you.

https://youtu.be/Gqt-eDS7wwc

Happiness

This is a big one for advertisers. Positivity drives connection and engagement with viewers. A 2010 study showed that the most emailed *New York*

Times articles were emotional and overwhelmingly positive (https://www.nytimes.com/2010/02/09/science/09tier.html?_r=0).

Example 2d

Subaru – "Happy"

This spot's title literally is "Happy." There's nothing but smiling faces set with a VO that also seeks to reassure us that having a Subaru is a guaranteed way of getting some happiness into our lives.

https://youtu.be/X9G3tIBidgg

Example 2e

Budweiser – "Wassup"

Debuting in 1999, the "Wazzup" campaign did everything right for viewers and became one of the most influential ideas in modern advertising. It's a simple premise. A bunch of dudes on the phone, speaking to fun, friendship, shared connections, and goofiness. We want to join in the fun.

https://youtu.be/3e4AHjCaiXw

Example 2f

Etsy – "Anything You Want"

The message here is simple: anything that makes you happy, you can find on Etsy. One of the on-camera talent actually mentions that things from Etsy come with love. What's happier than that?

https://youtu.be/cMmZ3v3JPW4

Confidence

Brands also seek to link themselves with the idea of

confidence. These spots often also touch on security because the two go hand in hand.

Example 2g

> Farmer's Insurance – "Hall of Claims Parking Splat"
>
> The story being told here is that no matter what happens, Farmer's will be the solution. They literally reassure us with their tag line, "We know a thing or two because we've seen a thing or two." This is delivered by the on-camera talent (a very well-cast J.K. Simmons), but could just as easily been done with a VO.
>
> https://youtu.be/Icg8dP4FHWo

Example 2h

> Old Spice – "Questions"
>
> This campaign was just absurd, but that's what

made it so great. Watching this caricature of manliness, we can't help but feel confident that if a guy uses Old Spice body wash, he'd take over the world and make his lady confident in their choice of man. Swan dive!

https://youtu.be/jyrW4JK6Lg8

Example 2j

Famous Footwear – "Converse Confidence"

They literally say they're selling confidence. I think that makes my point.

https://www.ispot.tv/ad/7Rou/famous-footwear-converse-confidence

Here's an assignment: start watching commercials, and look for the way of being or state of mind they're pitching. Listen to the copy delivered by the on-camera talent and the VO. Pay attention to the big picture, and try to see how the voice fits in. Notice how many celebrities or athletes you see and hear. They're our competition, but we shouldn't look at them in an adversarial way. They're hired because they bring something unique to the performance. If we can define what that is, we might be able to bring some of it to our reads.

Chapter Three

Building a Framework

Let's set about the business of building reads that have a positive impact on the creative team. Remember, we have two objectives. We need to show them you understand what they're going for, and we want them to experience the emotion they expect their audience to feel.

The Commercial Talent's Mindset

Think of commercials as stories that just happen to be thirty seconds long. Like every good story, they have a beginning, a middle, and an end. Not every commercial script is written in a way that makes it easy to tell where those sections are, but many are written in exactly that way.

That mindset, of being a storyteller first and foremost, gives you a place to start even when the copy isn't written in an obvious story format or when you can't relate to the product. I know it's tough to pull a whole story out of a few sentences, especially when there doesn't seem to be much information to go on. But trust me when I say that in those situations, storytelling will save you.

I'd always place storytelling ahead of communicating. Thinking of yourself as a communicator is just not specific enough, and it doesn't give you anything to go on. When we deliver commercial copy, we have to know who we're talking to. I'm a visual learner, so I actually picture a person who might want to hear the message in the spot. Somehow, "I'm going to communicate with you" doesn't give me as much ammunition as "You've got to hear this great story."

Plus, thinking of yourself as a communicator is outdated thinking. It doesn't align with what advertisers are looking to do in today's marketplace. There isn't a brand in the world that spends top dollar to communicate. Today's marketers want to tell stories.

Since video is a visual medium, our job as voice talent is to support the visual story being told. We're often secondary to the picture, but not always. The talent who can tell the difference will do very well with those in charge of the casting process.

Building Context

Learning how to interpret and deliver ad copy is like trying to hit a target that's always moving. No two spots are the same, yet our goal is always the same: to deliver the best read possible. How can we do that when the scripts are always changing?

Just as all good stories have a beginning, middle, and end, there's one thing all good storytellers have: an opinion. You can tell their point of view on what's happening in the story as they tell it. Without an opinion, the story's just flat—it doesn't come up off the page.

To form a point of view, we need some context, a framework within which to work. There are three bits of information that are perfect for giving us a starting point. I call them macros because they give us a birds-eye view of where the creatives are coming from. Surveying the spot from a high level allows us to discover things about it before we've read a single word of the script.

1. The Industry

Ever notice that commercials for jewelry are almost

universally soft and fuzzy? That truck commercials have a gritty and tough feel? Our first touch point for context comes from the industry to which the spot's product or brand belongs.

It doesn't matter if the story being told is hilarious or heartwarming, the industry will almost always dictate the general character of the voice over. The tech industry always wants their voices to sound smart. If you're doing a medical spot, you'd do well to have some empathy in your read. If it's a kids' product, the voice is going to be fun unless the product is for babies, which usually requires a much warmer read.

Creatives almost universally ask their talent to sound trustworthy, but that's going to sound different depending on the industry. For example, trustworthy in the wealth management industry usually sounds male and leans toward the mature side. The beauty industry usually relies on younger female voices.

COMMERCIAL VOICE OVER STRATEGIES

Why the difference? Every advertiser aims to create spots that connect with their customers, whom they know very well. Older customers are the wealth management industry's bread and butter because they're traditionally the demographic that has a need for those products. The beauty industry thrives on fantasy and glamour, concepts that are strong with younger female customers.

On the other hand, you'll hear voices of all ages and types in fast food spots because their customer profile is literally anyone who can spend a few bucks on lunch. Whatever the industry, the job will be won by the talent who best reflects the audience the client is trying to reach.

There are exceptions. There isn't one single way to describe the perfect voice for any particular industry, and it's true there are plenty of male voices doing beauty and female voices doing wealth management spots. But brands, especially big ones, tend to move in a very narrow lane. They like to stick with what works.

As part of your research, head to iSpot.tv and look up an advertiser and their competitors and see if you can detect some patterns. For example, I bet you'll notice that the travel industry usually wants an aspirational voice.

2. The Brand Itself

The bigger the brand, the more likely they are to do the same thing over and over again. That's reflected in the reads their talent deliver in their spots. If you get an audition for a large legacy brand, listen to the talent on their past commercials and know that they're not going to waver much from that formula. Don't reinvent the wheel; do what you hear in their other spots.

Smaller brands are more willing to push against the traditions of their industry. They may view themselves as trendsetters and might look to reinvent an old convention. Hopefully, you'll be told if that's the case in the audition specs, or notes about the kind of voice the client is looking for that come with the audition. If not, lean toward reads that are common to their industry and their past work.

3. The Audience

Of all the things to consider when we get a new audition, the spot's target audience is possibly the most important. The audience is the silent partner in the commercial. They may not be in the planning meetings, but they have a great amount of influence over the spot. This makes them important to both creatives, who are trying to grab their attention, and talent, who are trying to speak to them.

Decision makers will always keep their target audience in mind when listening to auditions. If the spot is targeting a certain demographic, talent who don't fit that group won't make the short list because the audience may not identify with them.

From the talent's point of view, knowing the audience is a huge help. Sometimes you'll get lucky and the specs will tell you who the intended audience is, but if they don't, you have to look for clues. Start with the subject matter. If the concept involves moms and babies, you can be sure you're talking to new moms.

The brand is the next best clue. Who do they usually speak to? Head to iSpot.tv or YouTube and check their past work because chances are they're trying to reach the same group. If you can't find any of their commercials, look for examples from competing brands.

As important as the audience is, it's not enough just to know you're talking to new moms as a whole. You might imagine yourself talking to a crowd of them, but that will lead to a very general read. We need to be more specific. Pick one mom and give her a face. Good storytelling is personal and much more effective one-to-one. So instead of talking to a group of people, talk to one person.

To accomplish this, cast someone from your real life as your audience and refer to them by name. I have a friend who lives in a crummy neighborhood, but he has a nice collection of high-end music gear. So if I get an audition for a home security product, I'm going to talk to him because I know he might actually be interested in the story.

If you don't know anything about the brand, the industry, or the audience, ad copy just amounts to some words on a page. Researching the macros will help, but to truly bring the spot to life, you'll have to look closer.

Chapter Four

Building the Read

To get a complete picture of what the creatives may be going for, we need to look at what I call the micros.

In contrast to the macros, which look at the larger picture, these are the details of the copywriting itself.

Every writer has their own style, but they all follow basic advertising principles. For example, they try to tell the story using the fewest words possible. Their message has to be specific, succinct, and single-minded.

Writers also use distinct styles of messaging to make their point. Over the years, I've found most spots fall into one of eight formats. I've seen them so often, I've given them names:

- Problem/Solution
- Retail
- Client Narcissism
- The Facts
- The Tag
- The Novel
- Play-by-Play
- The Abstract Phrase

Each category has its own unique tells and traits. Let's have a look at them.

Problem/Solution

This format always starts with a problem, followed by

the solution. The problem is stated up front, and the solution (the product, service, or brand) gets most of the attention in the rest of the spot. For talent, that almost always means talking down the lines referring to the problem and talking up the client.

Example 4a

> Everything that your family touches during the day sticks with them.
>
> Make sure the germs they bring home don't stick around.
>
> Our disinfecting products kill germs that can live on surfaces up to 48 hours.
>
> You handle life. We'll handle the germs.

The problem is germs and how long they stick around. The implication is that the longer your family is exposed to them, the worse it is for your health. The solution is the product, which kills those nasty germs, eliminating the risk of getting sick. Pretty straightforward.

Retail

Car and truck brands, furniture stores, supermarkets, and many other retail businesses like to use this format.

Example 4b

> It's the Hyundai year-end sales event.
>
> With great deals on the all new Tucson.
>
> Elantra.
>
> Santa Fe.
>
> And the groundbreaking Kona.
>
> All backed by America's best warranty.
>
> Get to your Hyundai dealer today!

Retail scripts are all about a deal or the sell, and it can be difficult to see a story in them. It helps to imagine an exclamation point at the end of every statement, even if there isn't one.

Client Narcissism

The hallmark of this category is the endless praise clients heap upon themselves. The copy contains nothing but wonderful things about their brand or product. At first glance, these are challenging because really, what can you do with a list of compliments?

Example 4c

> You have to be different to make a difference.
>
> So we are.
>
> We exist only to benefit those whom we serve.
>
> Every decision we make, we take as an opportunity to move higher.
>
> We grow, innovate, and push boldly forward.

> And find new ways to pursue excellence through better outcomes.
>
> It's our innate desire to serve and relentless resolve to perform that enable us to impact the lives of millions.
>
> We are CARMOR. And we work for you.

Finding ways to make subtle changes in your attitude will help you here, as will the industry and the brand's past work or the ads of their competitors.

The Facts

Copy written in this genre is usually devoid of anything but facts. In this example, there's a little sell, but the rest of it is just stuff the advertiser thinks you should know. Simple, almost monotone, reads work well here.

Example 4d

> The Rugged. All new, always up for the job.

> With an intelligent four wheel drive system unmatched in its ability to detect wheel spin. The torque biasing limited slip front differential mechanically multiplies brake force by over three times, lending it to the wheel with more grip.
>
> Giving the Rugged the most advanced four wheel drive system in the industry.
>
> The Rugged. Always up for the job.

There's still a story being told here, even though at first glance it seems like there isn't one. The trick is to look past the laundry list of items in the description of the product.

The Tag

Tags are short and come at the end of a spot like they've been tagged on, hence the name. This category can include actual tags, but there are also plenty of spots with announcer lines that might as well be. A great example would be a long-running campaign from Southwest Airlines. Every spot was different, but at the end of each one there came a "ding" and a VO would say:

Example 4e

You are now free to move about the country.

That guy had the best job in VO because he recorded that phrase once, and it was used for years without him ever setting foot into a recording studio for Southwest again. A tag isn't a throwaway line, and it is always based in the story being told. Look to the rest of the spot and match your delivery to the attitude you find there.

The Novel

This is my favorite category because it allows for some really good storytelling.

Copy in The Novel is well written and beefy. These

usually work best as sixty-second spots and are often recorded that way, then cut into shorter versions later. There is usually a lot of material to chew on.

Example 4f

> Some days, you feel like you can conquer the world.
>
> Other days, you can't get out of bed.
>
> Some days, you're on top.
>
> Other days, your whole world's upside down.
>
> Some days, life gets the best of you.
>
> And you just need a hug.
>
> So when you get knocked down,
>
> Get right back up and find the meaning of life.
>
> Go ahead. Sing out loud.
>
> Be yourself.

> Make a new friend.
>
> Embrace that bad hair day.
>
> Smile big, stick together, and value every day.

TV spots that are driven by the VO, like many of the spots I make videos about on my YouTube channel, are Novels.

Play-by-Play

Male voice talent will see these come along pretty often. Play-by-play scripts are written in the style of sports announcers, from the quiet reads of golf commentators to bombastic over-the-top soccer announcers. No trick here except to sound like you're announcing the sport that's written into the script.

Example 4g

> Gary is one for two, and he steps up to the register.

Last time he swung for the double play and hit it out of the park.

He knew every time his team turns a double play, the next day all double cheeseburgers are just a dollar.

Heck of an effort, let's see what he's got up his sleeve this time.

And the pitch...

Oh no! He dropped his wallet.

That'll go down as an error.

The Abstract Phrase

You can tell you're working with this category when your lines don't all seem to be connected in any meaningful way. Instead they're a collection of seemingly unrelated statements. You simply must find a story to tell, even if you invent different stories for different lines.

Example 4h

> Will you be one of them?
>
> The ones who stand up.
>
> Stand and deliver.
>
> The ones who won't go quietly.
>
> Headwinds? Don't care.
>
> Uphill battle? Bring it.
>
> Like a force.
>
> Like THE force.
>
> Take a stand.

Being able to categorize the kind of spot you're reading simplifies the process of building your reads and, really, your entire commercial career. If you can get a handle on these eight formats, you're golden.

I estimate that about 80 percent of the auditions in my inbox fall into these categories, and I'm very comfortable in all of them (except the Abstract Phrase, which hates me). You never want to standardize your reads for any type of work, but you definitely want to be familiar with what works for each.

The Three Act Structure

You don't have to be an actor or writer to know that stories often work best when they're told in three parts. The beginning introduces us to the world of the story and the characters who live in it. The middle might give us a conflict along with more pieces of the story's puzzle before coming to the third part, the end, where we get some kind of resolution.

Most commercials are written the same way. They follow a three act structure, though obviously the acts are much shorter. There's also one other big difference: they're missing landmark events that tell us where those acts begin and end.

Long-form narratives rely on events to push the story forward. Without them, the story wouldn't have anywhere to go. Take James Cameron's 1997 film, *Titanic*. In Act 1 we see the boat in all its gilded glory, we meet Jack and Rose, and we witness the clash between rich and poor. Rose, miserable with her life and the idea of marrying a man she doesn't love, decides to chuck it all. Spotting her preparing to jump into the ocean, Jack talks her down, which is the first event because it brings Jack and Rose together. In Act 2 we get to see their relationship blossom into a romance. Rose decides to ditch everything and go with Jack, then BAM! Iceberg, the second event. Act 3 is about survival and we all know how the movie ends.

This is an oversimplification of the story, but you can see that it can be broken down into three parts, separated by major events without which the story couldn't move forward. We typically don't get identifiable events in commercials, so to find the acts, we need other clues. Look at the previous examples. Any of them, with perhaps the exception of The

Tag, can be divided into three acts. Take another look and listen to Example 4a.

> Everything your family touches during the day sticks with them.
>
> Make sure the germs they bring home don't stick around.
>
> Our disinfecting products kill germs that can live on surfaces up to 48 hours.
>
> You handle life. We'll handle the germs.

This spot is five sentences long, but we can divide it up by looking at the content of each one. The first line sets up the world we're in. It introduces a character (a family) and sets up their problem: they have to deal with harmful germs all day. That's exactly what the first act of a movie would do, so we'll make it Act 1.

In lines two and three we learn there's something the family can do about their problem, a solution that lasts much longer than you'd think. That's a surprise, otherwise known as a plot twist. The copy also tells us to make sure germs won't stick around. This is a call to action, a very common element in spots, but the placement here is a little unusual because they usually come in the final act. We'll make these two lines our Act 2.

That leaves the last two lines. The first flatters us by saying we're just fine, we're going to handle life. Who handles life? People who really have their stuff together. That must be us! Then they reassure us by saying we'll be safe from those nasty germs if we use the product. These last two sentences are a second call to action, though less obvious than the first. It's the closest thing we're going to get to a resolution of our story, so we'll make those two lines Act 3.

Now take another look at and listen to Example 4b.

> It's the Hyundai year-end sales event.
>
> With great deals on the all new Tucson.

Elantra.

Santa Fe.

And the groundbreaking Kona.

All backed by America's best warranty.

Get to your Hyundai dealer today!

This example requires a little more imagination. There are no characters and no obvious elements that define a traditional story, but we can still break it down into three parts.

Like the first example, the first act is compressed into the first line. It tells us where we are and lets us know what to expect. Lines two through six make up Act 2, where we get what Act 1 promised. The final line is our call to action, Act 3.

I'll admit, this is a stretch. There's no conflict, no events, nothing but a list of vehicles. But if you approach this copy as just a list, you're not booking this job. The decision makers expect to tell a story, and the three act structure helps immensely.

In *Titanic,* each act has a distinctive attitude, a way the audience is supposed to feel. Act 1 is uplifting and hopeful as we see these engaging young characters discover an amazing ship. Act 2 appeals to our romantic side as we begin to root for Rose and Jack, our new onscreen best friends. Then the story abruptly rips those comfy feelings away as the ship sinks, and in Act 3 we gasp along with them as they fight to stay alive. Those are all very different kinds of energy.

We can apply the same logic to our car commercial. If each act of the spot is going to have a different energy, that has to come from somewhere. We don't have events or life and death conflicts, so it's up to us to fill in those blanks. We can do this by borrowing a concept from stage acting: intentions.

When an actor talks about intentions, they're trying to discover what's behind the things a character is saying or doing. For any given moment in a story, actors find possible intentions through all kinds of script analysis techniques. They've got the luxury of working with much longer narratives, so they have more details to mine for inspiration.

In commercials we don't get much background, but we can decide why we're saying what we're saying by using the things we know: the industry, the brand, the product, the ad's concept, and the audience. Plus, we know that advertisers don't sell things; they sell ways of being and states of mind.

To prep for this Hyundai spot, I'd look at the audition specs, consider the storyboards if they're included, watch some of Hyundai's past work, and probably settle on selling excitement. In fact, I'd go with excitement even if there were no specs, boards, or past work to see. Why? Because this is just like a thousand other car spots I've seen before, and they're pretty much all selling excitement. It's a safe bet unless the specs tell me otherwise.

However, that's kind of a trap. It would be easy to just whip yourself into a frenzy and shout this copy to the rooftops, a choice that would make you sound like a lunatic. You can't just do one level of excitement throughout the whole thing. Listen to Example 4i to hear what I mean.

Example 4i

> It's the Hyundai year-end sales event.
>
> With great deals on the all new Tucson.
>
> Elantra.
>
> Santa Fe.
>
> And the groundbreaking Kona.
>
> All backed by America's best warranty.
>
> Get to your Hyundai dealer today!

Everything! Is! Excruciatingly! Exciting! That's not storytelling. So let's look at this copy again. Act

1 is the intro. Set up the world of the spot by starting with some strong excitement. Let listeners know that this world, this alternate reality, contains shiny objects that move, and that's amazing.

Example 4-j

> It's the Hyundai year-end sales event.

Now in Act 2, back off on the excitement just a bit because we've seen your version of reality, and we like it. Now we want to know more. If you're shouting at us, we won't listen or learn anything. So educate us more than excite us.

Example 4-k

> With great deals on the all new Tucson.
>
> Elantra.
>
> Santa Fe.
>
> And the groundbreaking Kona.

All backed by America's best warranty.

Finally, for Act 3, close the deal with some authority and urgency. You've earned that right. We like your shiny, spinning objects, and we want to be as stoked about them as you are.

Example 4-1

Get to your Hyundai dealer today!

Consistency is boring to our ears, and it's boring in storytelling. Can you imagine if a musician looked at a piece of music and decided to ignore what's written and just play one note, over and over? Variation is what makes the music pleasing to hear. Same thing with our reads. That's where the acts come in. Use them to vary your intentions, which will vary the energy of your reads.

Dividing commercials into chunks helps you speak the copywriter's language. They're expecting different colors, attitudes, intentions, whatever you'd like to call them, in different parts of their scripts. If you deliver them, you'll be on their short list. If you don't, they'll click right through your audition.

CHAPTER FIVE

Breaking down Copy, Part I

When we're sent an audition, we get a script and a few bits of information, and then we record. To keep our audition from being a shot in the dark, we need to bring everything together: the macros, micros, all the information we can extract from what we're given. In this chapter, we'll go step-by-step through the process of breaking down a new piece of commercial copy. Here's our first example.

COMMERCIAL VOICE OVER STRATEGIES

Television Commercial

WRITER/AD	TITLE Harrys Orange Shake	VERSION
DATE	LENGTH	STATUS
OFFICE	CLIENT Harrys Custard	BUY
JOB NUMBER	ISCI CODE	MASTER NUMBER
PRODUCER	OC TALENT	VO TALENT
MUSIC/SINGER		

Casting note: *male 50s. Everyman, yet a voice of experience.*

The past. An ice cream truck comes down an idyllic suburban street on a hot summer day.

VO: Remember when you were a kid, and you'd chase the ice cream truck?

Several boys and girls run down their driveways toward the truck, which slows to a stop.

A boy gets an orange push pop and runs to a backyard treehouse. As his friends join him, we see their treats are melting already.

VO: All that sprinting and panting just to get an orange cream pop that would melt down and make your hands all sticky.

Later, the ice cream's gone and the boy sits next to a pigtailed girl. He shyly tries to hold her hand.

VO: Then when you went to hold Robin Swanson's hand, she got grossed out and called you "Sticky Hands Steve."

We see her recoil and look at her hand, which is now sticky. Our VO matches the her mouth movements as she insults the boy. Steve is mortified. She leaves as the other kids laugh.

Cut to the present day, a man walks into a Harry's. Cut to him ordering at the counter, getting an Orange Cream Shake.

VO: Well now there's the Orange Cream Shake from Harry's. Made with our signature custard, it's the perfect blend of orange and cream...in a cup.

And walking happily out the front door, past a woman who's dressed like the girl from the treehouse.

Our guy gives her an easy smile. She smiles back with a look of...do I know that guy?

SUPER: Harry's logo splash

VO: Harry's Custard. The taste that takes you back.

Step 1: Read Everything Available

When you get a new piece of copy, read everything on the page. A lot of people just look at the VO lines, but don't make that mistake. Taken together, the on-camera action, stage directions, the lines the on-camera actors have (if there are any), and specs from casting provide a starting point for how you'll tell this story. Even if the VO consists of a single line at the end of the script, your best read is only as good as your overall understanding of what the creatives are trying to accomplish.

This script has three elements to consider: the on-camera action, the VO, and the audition specs. The action and the VO together allow us to picture what the spot's going to look like. We can imagine the story playing out shot by shot, since it's spelled out on the page. Maybe the footage of the kids has an old-timey filter applied so it looks different than the present-day scenes with the adults.

The only thing missing might be the style of music the creatives intend to use. We're rarely given that information, so we'll proceed without it. If they tell us, though, we can grab it and read the audition with it playing in the background. One thing: only use music for inspiration. Don't let it bleed onto your audition. All auditions should contain your voice only. No music or sound effects allowed. Ever.

Step 2: Narrow down the Way of Being or State of Mind

Remember, advertisers don't sell stuff; they sell ways of being and states of mind. This spot leans heavily on nostalgia, which appeals to our longing for the way things used to be. It's interesting because typically nostalgic spots frame the past in a positive light and prompt us to take action today in response to our warm, fuzzy feelings of yesterday.

But in this case, the past has some awkwardness to it though it's still kind of charming since the story is relatable. The way of being and state of mind comes from what actually happens and is said in the spot. If we break this commercial down into a one-sentence summary, it would be something like "Grown-up finally gets to enjoy his favorite childhood treat without making a fool of himself." If you can finally have something in a way that lets you have all the positive parts of it (the taste) without the inherent negative parts of it (the mess), then what makes you go out and get that thing?

The product solves that problem. It lets you have something you love without the inconvenience and embarrassment that comes with it. You can finally get it all, flavor and portability without cleanup. You can be confident in your choice of dessert. So on a broad note, this spot is selling confidence.

Step 3: Consider the Macros

Look at the commercial on a macro level. Consider the industry, brand, and product in the spot. If you've never been to a Harry's Custard, look them up and find out who they are. In reality, I made up the brand for this book, but the copy is modeled on an actual spot produced by a national fast food chain. If Harry's were real, you'd probably find some of their commercials on their corporate website, YouTube, or iSpot.tv, and you'd use those reads as a starting point for your own.

Let's say your research tells you Harry's Custard is a burger chain. Try to see how they position themselves in the crowded fast food industry. They emphasize their desserts. People visit Harry's for the custard; the burgers are secondary. That explains why they're doing an entire spot on one dessert item.

The product is an orange cream shake, a new (or maybe it's an old standby) dessert they're offering. It's a treat, probably not something a customer would get every time they order lunch, but maybe it's an item for which they'd make a special trip, especially on a hot day. It's a good bet they'll run this spot over the summer.

Step 4: Identify the Audience

The script gives us our first clue about the audience. It opens with kids enjoying a treat, but in the end, we see an adult visiting a Harry's to pick up a shake. That's our audience, and the spot is using a funny little story to relate to them.

Who doesn't have an awkward moment from their childhood? And how many of us wish we could go back and show the person who was part of that moment that, as an adult, we've got it together? I can relate to that, and so can millions of other grown-ups.

The audition specs give us another clue. They call for an older voice, one with experience. When I read this script, the overall message I get is that I can have something I loved as a kid, especially now that it will fit into my current lifestyle. Having an older, reassuring voice deliver that message infuses it with more credibility than we'd get from a younger voice. Mature voices are those of experience and are frequently the choice for a spot playing on nostalgia. I'm going to guess Harry's Custard is talking to adults who still love to treat themselves now and then. That's pretty much everyone, which is dangerous since we need to personalize the story.

You could choose to identify your audience as "adults over thirty," but really, what does that tell you about them? And even if you knew a lot about that group, how would you address them? You'd lecture them because that's what we do when we talk to large groups. Lecturing is a no-no in advertising.

Your reads will be far more effective if you picture yourself telling the spot's story to one person. Cast someone from your real life. Think about the people you know, someone who matches up with the intended demographic and might actually be interested in what you have to say. Get the words up off the page by having a conversation with them.

Step 5: Get Micro

Does this spot fit into one of the eight most common types of spots? Let's look.

Example 5a

> Remember when you were a kid, and you'd chase the ice cream truck?
>
> All that sprinting and panting just to get an orange cream pop that would melt down and make your hands all sticky.
>
> Then when you went to hold Robin Swanson's hand, she got grossed out and called you "Sticky Hands Steve."
>
> Well now there's the Orange Cream Shake from Harry's.

> Made with our signature custard, it's the perfect blend of orange and cream...in a cup.
>
> Harry's Custard. The taste that takes you back.

The copy starts by asking us to think back to a fun time in a kid's life. If you had an ice cream truck in your neighborhood, you probably went running after it. Unless you have some horrible phobia of ice cream trucks, this automatically puts us in a pleasant state of mind.

But then the story takes a turn into uncomfortable territory. We get sticky hands, and we're teased for them. Reassuringly, we find out we don't have to deal with that anymore. We can have this shake and not worry about embarrassing ourselves.

This is a classic Problem/Solution format. Problem? This awesome treat makes an embarrassing mess in front of important people. The solution? The awesome treat has been re-engineered to take away the mess and the embarrassment. Plus, we can multitask while we enjoy it. You can't drive when your hands are covered in ice cream.

Step 6: Find the Acts

Dividing this spot into acts is tricky. We have a couple of choices. One option is to count the first sentence as Act 1, the second and third sentences as the second act, and the rest as Act 3. The logic is, the first statement sets up the spot's scenario, the conflict/problem is presented in Act 2, and the solution is revealed in Act 3. I like this method, but there's another way to look at it.

What if the first two sentences are Act 1, since they introduce the setup and present the problem? That would make the third sentence Act 2. That makes sense, since it's the one that is emotionally different from the rest of the spot. It's where the embarrassment lives. Act 3 reveals the solution and would go from, "Well now there's..." to the end. This way works, too.

The point is that no matter where those divisions are, your intentions must shift with them. It doesn't matter how you divide up the copy as long as your attitudes and approach make sense for what's being said or done. In this case, it's all sunshine and roses in the beginning until the sticky hands, then we hit some middle-school awkwardness, then we're back to the sunshine since we've solved this kid's problem. Tag on a call to action at the end, and you're done.

By going through these steps, you'll have everything you need to build a read that fits with the spot and brings it to life. You are no longer flying blind.

Chapter Six

Breaking Down Copy, Part II

This way of doing things, building a performance through thinking big and going small, can be used on any commercial audition in your inbox. But sometimes you won't have as much information as our previous example. The Harry's Custard spot had characters, a relatable story, an emotional hook, and an ending that wrapped everything up with a nice bow. Even if you're not used to breaking copy into acts or varying your intentions, you can still pull out a decent read with well-written copy.

Some copy, though, won't make it that easy on you. I'm thinking of my personal VO nemesis, The Abstract Phrase. It took me a long time to make friends with this kind of spot. How copywriters think throwing a bunch of unrelated statements together can work as a commercial, I'll never know. But they keep doing it, so I guess it works for someone. The secret to taming The Abstract Phrase is knowing that it only seems like the phrases are unrelated when you look at them on paper. In reality, they are very much connected to a larger story.

As if we didn't have enough to think about with this kind of script, there's often another wrinkle that makes it even tougher to figure out what's going on. The desire for secrecy among marketers means fewer and fewer auditions come with storyboards, pictures or descriptions of what's going on visually. We'll just get text, and anything else we normally use for background is missing. In extreme cases they won't even tell us the product or the brand.

In the Abstract Phrase, the story's going to be in the visuals, which we'll be supporting. But since we don't know what those look like, we'll have to start with what we know and manufacture the story ourselves. Let's take a look at an example.

Example 6a

>Product: *Beauty*
>
>Specs: *Our voice is confident, accomplished, on the younger side of middle age (early 30's-40s). She tells it like it is without winking or irony. Not sell-y. Storyteller. Celeb references are Serena & Venus Williams or Eva Longoria.*
>
>COPY:
>
>Start backward and end where you want to begin.

Finding it is half the adventure.

The one that led you here.

Here.

Here.

It was just your dream.

And yet all winding roads lead you back.

Like all our examples, this isn't exactly what was aired by a big brand, but it's pretty close. Only the big national advertisers do this kind of work, so these are good-paying jobs if we can book them.

Let's build a story. We're given two big clues about what this creative team is hoping to find: the industry and some celebrity references. I'd rather have everything else, but if we can only have one thing, the industry is possibly the best fact to know. Can you imagine if they didn't tell us that? We could be talking about anything—cloud software, booze, or bowling balls.

The nod to celebs is useful too. We can get a few hints from the names they mentioned. To build a story, let's go through the steps we learned so far.

Step 1: Read Everything Available

There's just not much to read. We've got a script, some specs, and that's it.

Here's what we know: it's a product in the beauty industry, they're looking for the voice of a woman who's confident and established but still young-ish. They've given us celebrity references that are pretty different from one another, not only in what they've accomplished but in their vocal quality. Venus and Serena Williams are champion tennis players, and Eva Longoria is a well-known actor.

The Williams sisters have voices that I would describe as a little more resonant and lower pitched, and when they speak, I hear them thinking things through and choosing words carefully. To me, Eva Longoria seems older than the sisters but sounds more youthful. She speaks at a quick pace and has a little vocal fry to her voice. That gives us quite the range.

We know that when it comes to our vocal quality, we have what we have. But in this case, our chances are equally as good at sounding like what the creatives hear in their heads if we have a higher-pitched voice or a lower one. It doesn't make much sense to dwell on that anyway, since the read is what's going to get us shortlisted, not the quality of our speaking voice.

Here's what we don't know: the brand, the product, or anything else. This opens up a couple possibilities. First, a well-known personality may be appearing in the spot, but the company hasn't announced the partnership. Or, the product line is new and hasn't been revealed by the brand. It's also possibe the spot has already been fully produced and the creatives don't like what they heard from their VO. Not wanting to embarrass anyone (especially if the read was originally done by the celeb in the spot), they're quietly looking for alternatives.

It's hard to know if any of these things are true, or if none are. But secrecy is always in place for a reason, especially in very competitive industries like beauty.

Step 2: Narrow Down the Way of Being or State of Mind

When I read this script, I detect a bit of a story thread, but not much. There are references to searching, or being on a journey. The fact that we're talking about adventures and winding roads definitely leads me to believe we're talking about striving for something. Is it literal? Is it a goal? Is it sports related, as in pushing yourself to be the best?

What seems to be consistent is this idea of being on a journey and finding your way back home. Home usually equates to security or comfort, but that doesn't seem right for a beauty product. People who are very accomplished become so by pursuing goals. That sounds like what we're talking about here, so I'm going with accomplishment as our state of mind.

Step 3: Consider the Macros

What do we know about the beauty industry? It's young, it chases trends, it relies on glamour and drama to sell confidence. It makes you want to be the best you that you can possibly be, and it gives you the tools to do it.

Head to iSpot.tv and YouTube and get familiar with the work of a few brands. There will be variations in approach. Cover Girl has a different look and feel than Neutrogena. Hunt for the brands that rely on the Abstract Phrase. Perfumes, luxury goods, and sports drinks are all common employers of this format.

While we're looking, find examples of the celebrity references doing VO. This should be easy, especially since iSpot lets you search by actor. To my ear, voice over reads done by the Williams sisters drip with confidence and accomplishment. I may be predisposed to have that impression since I'm a tennis fan, but that's what I get, and in this case, I would lean into it. You may hear something else, but the point is those references are there for a reason, so use them.

Step 4: Identify the Audience

The industry and celebrity references make it seem safe to assume we're talking to women. It appears we're shooting for the middle of the adult age range. I don't think we're talking to the young adult or senior crowd.

It's not a good idea to fall into the trap of speaking to "Women in their thirties and forties," so let's get more specific. Since we don't know the product, this is where we can use a combination of the copy and our imagination. The story is pretty clearly about going out there, finding something, and coming back. Is it a business? A relationship? Yourself? Who knows. But to find our audience, we need to pick something. Before I settle on exactly who I'm talking to, I'm going to need more information.

Step 5: Get Micro

It's obvious what kind of format we're dealing with. The Abstract Phrase is the only category for this kind of copy. One thing about The Abstract Phrase is that the subject matter is never trivial. This format is reserved for heady stuff: finding limits and pushing past them, risking everything for a goal, giving up things mere mortals wouldn't to gain something more valuable in return. This is not a story about making a peanut butter and jelly sandwich. Although if it was, that would be hilarious, and if any copywriters out there take that idea and run with it, consider yourself obligated to hire me as the VO.

Step 6: Find the Acts

I'm going to make the first line Act 1. It sets up our expectations by referencing the start of a journey, and it gives us some advice, which is a hint. That means whoever we're seeing visually has enough status and credibility to make such a statement because whatever it is, they've done it and can speak about it. I'm going to include the rest of the spot in Act 2 except the last line, which I'll call Act 3. The lines in Act 2 make me imagine a lot of different shots, like physical locations, or stages of a career, or even stages of a life. Act 3 signals the end of the story by implying that we come back to wherever we were before.

Now that I have all the information I'll ever get, I need to make some predictions and invent a story of my own, one that fits with what I know. Here goes.

The creatives are going to use strong visuals to tell a story about accomplishment. It's going to be told cinematically, with great cinematography and style. It'll star a female personality who's very successful, and the client wants to link her accomplishments, or at least her work ethic, with the product. The purpose of the story is to motivate and inspire women to grind through the mundane in search of greatness, just like the star of the spot. We'll feel proud of her, we'll wonder how she got where she is, and we'll lean in as she tells us.

Because of the reference to the Williams sisters, I could set the story in the world of sports. An athlete-chases-dreams-to-become-world-champion kind of thing. But whenever you come up with the story on your own, I suggest creating the story you'd want to watch. Listeners can smell insincerity a mile away, so if you don't buy into what you're saying, they won't either, and you won't be short listed for that audition.

Here's something about me: I'm personally less motivated by sports greatness than I am by people who overcame great hardships to become successful in whatever they aimed for, so I'd skip the sports world and build a story around something else. The story you build has to work for *you* since it's *your* audition.

For some reason, when I hear this script in my head, I see a female veteran who was wounded in service to her country, clawing herself back to normalcy through the hard work of physical therapy. I see scenes of her struggling to adapt to a prosthetic limb, conquering it so it becomes a part of herself. Then I see shots of her trying new things, picking up new skills and starting a business, or teaching others.

In the end, her path takes her somewhere she never thought she would go, yet she's still the same person she was when she first enlisted. The injury actually turned out to be the thing that got her where she wanted to be all along, and we admire her for the positive impact she's had on others. It's all about the journey and her can-do attitude. And she looks great doing it because the product is subtly woven in.

These images are so strong for me that I can hear the music the creatives would choose to go along with them. I can see the slow-mo shots, the drone footage, and the quick edits. That's when you know you've got a good story on your hands, one that works for you. It doesn't matter if it's not the story the actual commercial will tell. You have no chance of guessing correctly. All you should worry about is being invested in the one you're telling, so you can deliver the best read possible.

This process is pretty simple. Gather all the facts, fill in the gaps with research, and draw the best conclusion you can, so you end up with a story you'd love to tell.

If you're thinking, "This seems like a lot to go through for a lousy commercial audition," I get it. It *is* a lot of work. And I'll say it again: this isn't the only way out there. If this seems to be a little much, know that after you do this awhile, pulling stories out of commercials will become easier.

But I would encourage you to give it a try because unless you're a commercial booking machine, you have nothing to lose. The worst that could happen is you have a better understanding of what you're being asked to do and what the creatives expect from their voice talent.

Being a voice talent comes with a certain amount of responsibility. I'm not trying to be dramatic; we're not saving lives, but we are helping to save jobs. As a viewer, you may think of commercials as annoying intrusions on your TV time. As a voice actor, you might think of them as a way to further your career and make some money along the way. Both might be true, but commercials really exist to keep people employed.

Without advertising, we wouldn't sell nearly the amount of goods and services that we do. We voice commercials in service to the overall economy. The revenue gained from sales keeps companies open, workers in their jobs, food on the table, and kids in Little League baseball. So you can look at spots however you like, but when I'm spending a long time trying to figure out what to do with a piece of copy, and I have six others waiting to be done, I try to remind myself that it's time to keep some people employed. When all else fails, if you can't develop a point of view on the story in the spot, go with this: time to save some jobs.

Book the Team

If you've been in this business any length of time, you know that for every job out there, you're one of many voice talent doing your best to book it. Creatives have no shortage of choices, and they often don't know which way they're going with a voice until they hear something that makes them say, "That's the one."

You can do all the copy analysis you want, spend

all the time you can, and obsess over the tiniest mouth click and errant breath. But in the end, there are many, many other factors figuring into who gets which job. Your read might be amazing, but if you're not the right gender, age, ethnicity, or vocal type the team is hoping for, you're not booking the job. Some writers only use talent they know and have worked with before. Some want to work with local voice actors; others don't mind if you patch into the session from two thousand miles away. There is just no way to guarantee you'll book any job.

But that shouldn't be your goal. Only someone who is uneducated about the industry would approach auditions thinking every one of them will turn into a booking. Instead, your goal should be to book the creative team. On-camera actors have a saying when they have a great audition but don't land the role. We say, "I didn't book the job, but I booked the room." This means they went into an audition room prepared and left knowing the decision makers were impressed with their work.

Booking the room is important because repeat business is the lifeblood of our careers. We want decision makers to have a positive experience, so they'll bring us back again and again. Sooner or later, one of those auditions will be perfect for us.

As voice talent, booking the creative team means consistently turning in auditions that are unique and true to the story being told. If you do that, you're going to get noticed by whoever is listening. When those talent buyers see your name on their list, they'll know they can count on you for great reads, which will put you ahead of those unknown. Eventually, you'll book something, and because you'll be so solid and directable in the session, you'll be hired again and again.

And that's how you build a career.

Chapter Seven

Marking Up Copy

Before we talk about marking up a piece of copy, we have to decide whether we're going to print out the copy or mark up a digital version on a screen. I'll point out a couple of things about each method.

If you ever book a session at a professional recording studio, you will almost always be handed a piece of paper. You should not count on having a tablet in the booth. Instead you'll find a paper script on a stand, a pencil, and a set of headphones. Maybe water. That's it.

I believe that at the beginning of your career, you should be printing scripts. I think having something tangible to work with makes it easier to connect with the story and really understand what the spot is about. Clearly the pros at the studios think the same. However, because you're already working on a screen at home, it's more convenient to skip printing your scripts.

Try both methods. You may find it faster and easier to mark up a paper script. I personally do not print scripts at home unless I'm doing a job with a client on the other end of the line. Speed is important in a session, and I find it quicker to mark scripts and make copy changes with paper and pencil. To mark up a script digitally, you need a screen and an app to view and physically mark the copy with a stylus, mouse or your finger. I know people who work this way. If that's you, have at it.

Regardless of how you view your scripts, when

you're first learning how to interpret ad copy, it's good to have reminders about the ideas you come up with or ones your client is asking you to try. Having a copy-marking system is a way of doing that.

However, I want to caution you. Don't look at a marking system as a way to skip the work we talked about earlier. It's a supplement, not a substitute. As you can tell, I'm all about telling stories. Deciding how to say your lines is not storytelling, much like getting one of those floor diagrams that tells you where to put your feet is not learning how to ballroom dance. Let the story tell you how to deliver the lines.

But a few simple marks are very helpful to have. You might already have your own marking system, but I'll share the one I use.

The Marks

I like to give my brain a visual reference for what I was thinking when I worked out how to tell the story. Here are the marks I use.

COMMERCIAL VOICE OVER STRATEGIES

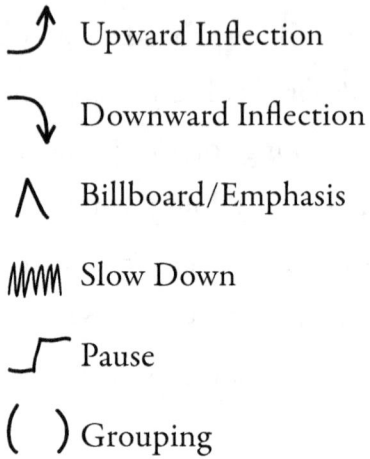

- Upward Inflection
- Downward Inflection
- Billboard/Emphasis
- Slow Down
- Pause
- Grouping

Upward Inflections

The upward inflection can be heard when a speaker's pitch goes upward at the end of the statement. This happens when we ask a question. Listen:

Example 7a

>   Did you get my message?

Here's how I mark up an upward inflection:

>   Did you get my message?

Upward inflections tell the listener that there's more information to come. When we ask a question, we anticipate an answer, so we go up with our voice to signal the listener that we expect them to respond. That makes them pay closer attention. We can do the same thing in commercials. It's a trick we can use to build anticipation when the copy doesn't allow for any. On my YouTube channel, I mention inflections pretty frequently in my copy analysis videos, so check them out for a ton of examples.

Downward Inflections

The downward inflection is the opposite of an upward inflection. It communicates finality. Listen:

Example 7b

> I left you a message.

Here's how I mark up a downward inflection:

> I left you a message.

Here's that same sentence, but delivered with an upward inflection.

Example 7c

I left you a message.

When delivered this way, it seems like there's more to be said, but I'm not saying it. That tricks the listener's ear to anticipate additional information. It's a good trick.

Downward inflections are statements, but they're a little more than that. They tell the listener we've come to the end of a thought, and there's nothing more to be said about it; we're going to move on to the next one. Copywriters usually expect a nice solid downward inflection at the end of lists and the end of spots. Downward inflections also signal authority. Sometimes that's what you want, other times not. Hit a downward inflection too hard, and you might sound a little on the preachy side. Like this:

Example 7d

Visit your local dealer today.

Soften it a little and the message isn't as forceful.

Example 7e

Visit your local dealer today.

Billboard/Emphasis

Sometimes writers want you to billboard, or emphasize, one word over the others in the sentence. This can sometimes seem unnatural, so instead of trying to remember which word I need to hit, I put an inverted "V" on it, like this:

Example 7f

That's how we do business.

If there are multiple words in a sentence they want me to billboard, I'll mark each one of them.

Example 7g

That's how we do business.

Slow Down

Most of the time, commercial copy moves at a pretty good clip. Pacing is brisk because often we don't have a ton of time to tell the story. Once in awhile, especially in longer spots, you have the time to slow down for emphasis. Or you can just vary your pacing for variety's sake. When I find a line I'd like to deliver slower than the rest, I mark it like this:

Example 7h

That's how we do business.

Pause

I'm going to guess that I've been given a million and one directions in my career. But the one that comes up most often is, "Can you take a little pause right there?" So I have a mark for that. It looks like this:

Example 7i

> We don't just heal the heart, we heal the human spirit.

You might notice there's a comma in this sentence, and the pause is right over the comma. Instinctually, you should want to pause here anyway, but I could also see a case for ignoring that comma, particularly if you're tight on time. The pause mark is the one I use most often, with the possible exception of the billboard mark.

This seems like a good time to talk about punctuation. There are two kinds of copywriters: those who care about punctuation and those who don't. The first kind is very invested in the voice talent following their punctuation and will wonder what's wrong with the ones who don't.

The second kind will just want to hear a good read, correct punctuation or not. There's really no way to know who wrote your audition copy or where their priorities lie, but in general, I recommend observing the punctuation unless it's way off. You'd be surprised how many "professional" copywriters will send out sloppy scripts. I've seen spelling mistakes, cut-and-paste errors, and my favorite, TEXT IN ALL CAPS, which makes me wonder if they want us to shout the whole thing. Most scripts are pretty clean, though, and I assume the writer is using punctuation as a guide to how they're hearing the script in their head.

Grouping

There's plenty of jargon in commercials, especially the further away from mainstream consumer goods you go. When you're voicing a spot for a four-wheeler or a skin care line, they're going to talk a lot about features and benefits. These can be tricky, and so can product descriptions. Sometimes you need to group multiple words together and treat the group as one thing. I just use parentheses. Example 5-4 has a bit of this. I'll separate out the offending line and let you listen to it here, first without grouping:

Example 7j

> The torque biasing limited slip front differential mechanically multiplies brake force by over three times.

And then with grouping:

Example 7k

> The (torque biasing limited slip front differential) mechanically multiplies brake force by over three times.

Hear the difference? Through grouping, you can convey that the individual words all go together and should be referred to as one big thing instead of multiple separate things. Grouping makes your life easier and makes you sound more like an expert than you actually are.

Now let's have some fun and mark up a whole new script. Here's a commercial script without marks.

> Tomorrow is a complete mystery.
>
> Every generation has tried to peer into it, to influence it, and predict what will unfold.
>
> What we know is that tomorrow is complicated.
>
> For every cure, there will be a new disease.
>
> For every peace, a new conflict.
>
> As we move forward, forces will work to pull us back.
>
> Testing our will, our commitment, and our dedication.

Tomorrow is not for one brand of expertise, or one way of thinking.

Tomorrow isn't a job for just anyone.

It's a job for us.

Now let's mark it up. I'm going to throw every mark I can think of into this script, so you can see how the full set could be used in an entire story. This is for demonstration purposes only. You don't want to have this much handwriting on your scripts. You definitely don't want to rely on them to give the read some kind of manufactured authenticity, or worse, get locked into one delivery because you marked it up a certain way. Use a pencil so you can easily change your mind.

COMMERCIAL VOICE OVER STRATEGIES

Tomorrow is a complete mystery.

Every generation has tried to peer into it, to influence it and predict what will unfold.

What we know is that tomorrow is complicated.

For every cure, there will be a new disease.

For every peace, a new conflict.

As we move forward, forces will work to pull us back.

Testing our will, our commitment, and our dedication.

Tomorrow is not for one brand of expertise or one way of thinking.

Tomorrow isn't a job for just anyone.

It's a job for us.

I threw every mark I could think of into this script, so you could see how the full set could be used in an entire story. This is for demonstration purposes only. You don't want to have this much handwriting on your scripts. You definitely don't want to rely on them to give the read some kind of manufactured authenticity, or worse, get locked into one delivery because you marked it up a certain way. Use a pencil so you can easily change your mind.

Let's go through each mark. I chose to set up the story by going a little slower through the first line. The extra emphasis makes listeners lean in a little more. The downward inflection at the end of the first line makes sense, since it's the first statement, the line that sets up the story. I'll make it a soft landing, though, to keep it from sounding too final.

In the next line, we get a very common characteristic of commercial copy: a group of three. A noun, in this case a generation, is described in a way that involves three verbs: peer, influence, and predict.

This technique of bringing three separate-yet-related things together is something we'll see again later in the script. You'll come across this in other commercials quite often.

You can handle groups of three in a couple of ways. You can go same, same, different, where you use the same inflection on the first two and give the last one the opposite inflection. You can also go same, same, same, where all of them get identical inflections. I think the first way is the safest under most circumstances, this one included. So we'll go up on "peer into it" and "influence it" and down on "predict what will unfold." It also makes sense to put a pause in between each item in the group, since it's likely that's how the writer is hearing it in their head.

Moving on, we're going to hit the word "know" in the next line, differentiating something definite from the idea in the previous line, which was uncertainty.

Then we'll go up on "cure" to give us somewhere

to go on "disease," putting a pause between them to separate them a bit. Same thing on the following line, bringing the dueling comparisons to an end with a downward inflection on "conflict."

Where are we going next? We're going forward, so we'll hit that word in the next line. And to drive home the point that this is hard work, we'll slow down for emphasis on "work to pull us back."

In the next line, we've got another set of three things: "will," "commitment," and "dedication." But this time we'll pause after the first and group the last two together, just to make it different from the earlier group of three. Variety lends interest to reads.

The emotional arc of the spot is coming to its peak, and we're going to heighten that by using upward inflections. Sometimes we can use them not to ask a question but to show listeners how passionate we are about a topic. We'll use them liberally on "expertise" and "thinking" as we lead into the penultimate line, where we can hit the word "anyone."

Because according to the spot, not just anyone can do this big, important thing we're talking about. We can emphasize that point with a little authority and a downward inflection.

And that brings us to the last line, the payoff of the whole story. I don't know what company this is for, but they really believe in themselves. In fact, they think they're possibly the only ones who can save us from this thing called "the future."

Whether you know the name of the company or not, it's clear they're framing themselves as capable and dedicated enough to take on the world's big challenges. We can help make that point by using one of the oldest commercial VO tricks in the book. We put a big fat pause in the last line and bring the last word downward as if to say, "End of story, thanks for listening, feel free to go about your business."

Have a listen to the final product (Example 71) and how all those marks show up in the performance.

CHAPTER EIGHT

The Matrix

You're now armed with all the information you need to build great commercial reads. It's the very process I've used to land dozens of high profile jobs in my career, ones that have paid a lot of bills. But I do want to say one more thing before you start applying all this knowledge.

You shouldn't expect to be good at this right away. If you are, good for you! You've been gifted with an amazing ability to translate ad copy into a language that listeners, professional and otherwise, identify with. I'm jealous.

But most of us are not born with this ability. It'll probably take a lot of practice. Like any skill, telling stories through ad copy requires time, patience, and especially familiarity. The more you do this, the easier it'll get.

At first, you have to be willing to be bad at it. I've laid that foot diagram on the floor for you, and you can put your feet where it says you should put them, but that doesn't mean you're dancing. To do that, you have to turn on the music and have some fun over and over again.

Do you remember that scene in the 1999 film *The Matrix*, where Neo (Keanu Reeves) is looking over Cypher's (Joe Pantoliano) shoulder at the screens with all the green code streaming by? It's the code that makes up the matrix. Cypher points to it and says, "You get used to it. I don't even see the code anymore. All I see is blonde, brunette, redhead."

That's what ad copy is like. When you're new to commercials, you just see all these words trying to sell stuff, and none of it is realistic because no one talks like that in real life. But it's a kind of code, and the skill of breaking it is very learnable. Just don't put too much pressure on yourself to get the hang of it right away.

Next Steps

In one of my other books, *The Voice Over Startup Guide: How to Land Your First VO Job*, I lay out seven steps to starting a career in VO, and the first step is to listen. I think you should do a lot of that. In fact, I think you should work backward and deconstruct the commercial reads that are making it to air. They're working for the creatives, so try to figure out why.

As you listen to a spot's VO, start by imagining the specs. Can you tell what vocal characteristics the team was going for when they sent out the audition?

Put a face to the voice in the spot and give them an activity. As they speak, are they leaning forward in their chair, or are they just waking up from a nap? See if you can break the spot into acts and if you can hear the energy shift as the read progresses. Listen for the amount of projection the talent uses. Are they shouting, or are they letting the mic do the work? Do you get the story being told? Are you able to see that the spot isn't trying to sell a product but to get us to feel a certain way?

It's like looking at a painting in a museum. When you first see the painting from across the room, there's something about it that draws you in, but you don't know how that artist created that image. So you move closer to see the brushstrokes. Only then can you get an idea of the mastery and skill required to make that painting. Start looking for the brushstrokes in commercial reads. You can find them if you listen.

This is what I do when I'm putting together

a VO analysis video for my YouTube channel. I reverse engineer spots because I want to see why they worked for the creatives. I want to figure out the story behind the story so that I can apply what I learn to my own auditions.

Then, practice turning that knowledge into a performance. You can start with the practice scripts in the next chapter.

Thanks for trusting me to show you all this stuff. I know you have a lot of choices about where to get your VO training, and I'm honored you chose this title.

Chapter Nine

Practice Scripts

Below is one script for every kind of spot mentioned in Chapter 5. All are based on actual scripts that have been auditioned and broadcast in the real world, though brand names have been changed. Find the acts, mark 'em up, and tell the story.

Problem/Solution

Nick was born to move.

Not necessarily after three toddlers with boundless energy.

But low back pain won't slow him down.

Because his doctor recommended America's number one pain reliever.

It targets the root of pain, and works all day long.

Leaving Nick with…maybe not as much energy as the triplets.

Look out world, Dad's back in charge.

America's number one pain reliever. Born to move.

Retail

Armand's biggest deals start tonight at 8 PM!

With exciting in-store door busters through Friday 1 PM.

Over 500 Big Buy specials.

Like pea coats, just $49.99. Men's sweaters, just $14.99.

It's our best Black Friday ever at Armand's.

Jingle more bells.

Client Narcissism

With the Harry's Footwear app I shop when I want, where I want.

I can redeem rewards anytime. I know the shoes my kids want.

'Cause I'm down with the hottest trends.

And I'm all about sharing my victories.

Yep, this summer, we're spending less time shopping for it, and more time owning it.

Amazing brands. Amazingly easy.
Harry's Footwear.

Victory is mine.

The Facts

Bordola is the only injection treatment for adults FDA approved specifically to correct sagging chin tissue.

You invest in your fitness, now invest in your profile.

Bordola, for moderate to severe fullness.

For a gradually improved chin profile.

Diminish your double chin with Bordola.

The Tag

These are short, so here's three of them.

Whatever tomorrow's technology, we'll make sure you're ready.

Complimentary drinks for two hours every night. Book now and save 20%.

Smart Storage. Helping you keep the things that matter most.

The Novel

Welcome to Sweet Street.

Where workers come to make delicious treats.

There's the baker of squares.

Next door to the sultan of spice.

And here's where confections are made by hand with delight.

And the last shop on the street is truly a treat.

It's the place where all the makers meet.

Together, these citizens of Sweet Street turn what they love into sweet ice cream treats.

Enjoyed by one and all.

The Artisan Collection.

from Harry's Ice Cream.

Play-by-Play

This one's so long, it's more of a Novel, but it sure is fun. Try doing it like a basketball announcer.

Jerry steps up to the fridge.

His choice of late-night snacks has been shaky lately, ever since that highly questionable pepperoni stick incident last Friday.

Let's see what he comes up with this time.

That huge container of leftover penne Alfredo is right in his field of view.

Behind it there seems to be an avocado. Not doing him any favors there.

He considers, eyes bouncing from avocado to Alfredo, ever the careful surveyor.

And there's his stomach, sending up the warning sign.

Alfredo, avocado, Alfredo, avocado.

Another growl from the stomach as if to say, "Not this time, Jerry."

Is that? Yes, it's the look of resignation crossing his face as he dives for the avocado in one of the best decisions he's made in a long time.

Proving once again there is such a thing as healthy snacks after midnight.

The Abstract Phrase

It's that trip we took.

Or all those weekends going nowhere.

It's whispers and our not-so-secret secrets.

It's that sparkle.

This gesture.

That glance.

It's that right there.

And this.

It's the memories we've made.

And the ones we're still making.

www.ingramcontent.com/pod-product-compliance
Lightning Source LLC
LaVergne TN
LVHW051524070426
835507LV00023B/3292